Discover The Circus

by Amanda Trane

© 2017 by Amanda Trane
ISBN: 978-1-53240-2692
eISBN: 978-1-53240-2708
Images licensed from Fotolia.com
All rights reserved.
No portion of this book may be reproduced
without express permission of the publisher.
First Edition
Published in the United States by
Xist Publishing
www.xistpublishing.com
PO Box 61593 Irvine, CA 92602

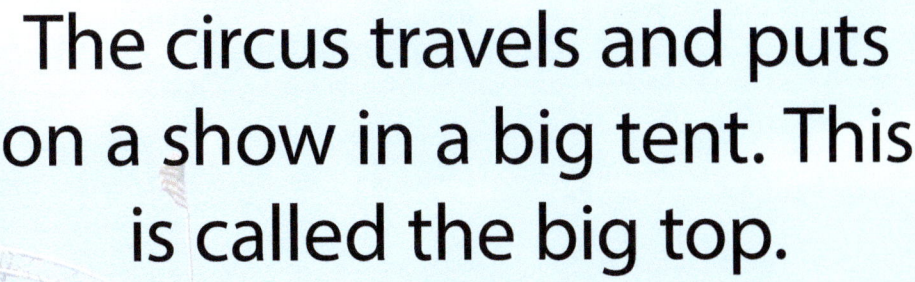

The circus travels and puts on a show in a big tent. This is called the big top.

Outside the big top, people play games. This is a test of strength.

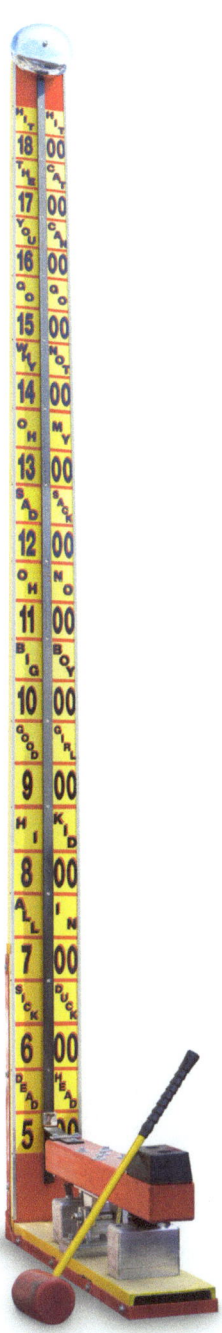

5

Some circuses have a carousel to ride. These horses go up and down in a circle.

Many people buy popcorn to take inside the big top.

The first people to perform are the clowns. This clown has big shoes.

This clown is jumping rope.

Some clowns can juggle.

Some clowns are silly.

This clown is riding a unicycle.

These are acrobats. They have good balance.

These acrobats are doing tricks in the air.

Some circuses have magicians who do tricks.

This man is a fire blower. He is very brave.

Many circuses used to have elephants do tricks.

Now, horses are the main animals found at the circus.

What would you like to see at the circus?

www.ingramcontent.com/pod-product-compliance
Lightning Source LLC
LaVergne TN
LVHW010021070426
835507LV00001B/27